LEARNING TO SEEK GOD'S PRESENCE

LEARNING TO SEEK GOD'S PRESENCE

by
Karen Pickering

LEARNING TO SEEK GOD'S PRESENCE

Copyright © 2014
Published by Pure Water Press, Kansas City, MO
PureWaterPress.com
purewaterpress@gmail.com

Edited by Sherrie Holman
Cover design by Andrea Loy
Layout and design by Jody Lokken

Printed in the United States of America

ISBN-13: 978-0692257180 (Pure Water Press)
ISBN-10: 0692257187

DEDICATION

This book is dedicated to my father, Eldien Edinger, who died 25 years ago. I still grieve the loss of his presence, but I rejoice that he is busy serving the Master he taught me to love all those years ago.

TABLE OF CONTENTS

ACKNOWLEDGEMENTS

The material on the following pages has been influenced greatly by two men I have never met. I have listened to Michael Card for years as a singer/songwriter and in more recent years as a teacher of deep biblical truth. The whole "Provision vs. Presence" concept I learned from him, and it is a key part of this material. Dr. Robert Kellemen is a biblical counselor, pastor and teacher. I have read most if not all of his books, all of which skillfully point hurting people to a wonderful God. I acknowledge both men as I have learned much from them and don't want to take credit for anything that originated with them. Ultimately, God is the one who is teaching me, and I am just repeating what I am learning as I sit at his feet.

Who is this study for? This is for someone in crisis: someone who has been through something that has shattered their world. This is for someone who is discouraged by the fallen world we live in and is yearning for something more. This is not for the Christian who has it all figured out or who has it all together. This is not about rules and being a better Christian. It is about finding the Creator in the here and now.

This is not a self-help course, a solutions manual, or a quick-fix for your problems. It is all about a new way of thinking which will lead to a new way of living. It is simply about God and learning to live in His presence. Someday we will live in His presence for eternity. He wants us to learn how to do it well before we arrive.

This study is not for the faint of heart. It will take hard work. Most of the work will come in the form of admitting your need and allowing God to do His work. This is not a study that will allow you to dwell on your past. Rather the purpose is to shift your focus from yourself to God. As you and a faithful friend complete each lesson prayerfully and thoughtfully, I pray God will transform your thinking and your life.

Notes before you begin.

•When I ask you to list the main characters, I mean human characters. God is an integral part of each of the stories we will look at, so it goes without saying that He is there in the midst of each story.

•You will find two lists at the back of the book. The first is "Who is God?" I would encourage you to note carefully what you learn about God through this study and other Bible reading that you may do throughout the week. You might want to use a separate notebook. I would also encourage you to continue the habit long after this study is over. We will never learn all there is to learn about God.

•The second list is "Who am I?" This is not a list of our good points or talents. It is about writing down how God sees us. What is our purpose? What does God enable us to do? Who are we to God? It is only through learning about the God who made us that we can finally understand our intended purpose and place. Our potential skyrockets the moment we understand that our worth originates with Him.

•This study is meant to be done with a discipleship partner. It can be done alone, but it will be more beneficial if you find a faithful friend who can work on this with you.

"All scripture is inspired by God and is useful for teaching the faith and correcting error, for re-setting the direction of a man's life and training him in good living. The scriptures are the comprehensive equipment of the man of God and fit him fully for all branches of his work." II Timothy 3:16-17 (Phillips)

A Tale of Two Surgeons

I sought out a surgeon to fix my broken ankle. He examined the bone, made a plan and scheduled the surgery. The surgery was uneventful. Things went as planned. They gave me four pages of very specific written instructions and the number to call if I had any trouble. They waved good-bye as my husband took me home. Within hours the trouble began.

It took two days for us to convince them there was a problem. I had an allergic reaction to the first pain killer. The second pain killer sent me into another tailspin and I was unable to eat more than a few spoonfuls at a time. By day three I was so weak I was having trouble communicating. Late into the third day, we called an ambulance and I spent five hours in the ER. They adjusted to my medications and sent me home. As my condition continued to decline, my family began to research, then came up with their own treatment plan. By day five, I was finally turning a corner. Through all of this we had called the doctor nine times; we usually got an answering machine. A receptionist would then call us back and forward our complaint. Half of the time they never called back. We talked to many nurses who were irritated at the frequency of our calls and assumed we were not following the plain instructions we had been given. We were told to call our pharmacist or our family doctor. In all of those conversations, not once did our surgeon call us back or speak to us on the phone.

My post-op appointment was scheduled for day nine. My husband mentioned to the surgeon that the recovery had been hard. "Yes," the surgeon responded, "I heard about all your trouble." Nothing more was said on that subject. He said things looked good, and he would see me in three weeks.

There is another surgeon who is the Great Physician. He sought me out. He sees the brokenness that I do not want to face. He lovingly insists on addressing the fractured pieces one by one; making the cuts, realigning the bones, making them whole and binding them tight. He has written a book of instructions and encouragement for me. He sits with me as I heal and watches over me as I sleep. He gently wipes my tears that fall from the pain of the procedure He is determined to see me through. He grieves over the painful work that must be done, but He presses on, never leaving me, bringing others to encourage and teach me through each operation. The process is slow, painful and hard, but The Surgeon is always with me and is carefully watching and adjusting as I respond to Him.

The first surgeon was skilled. He did the job he set out to do. I sought the provision of his skill and he obliged. The second surgeon offers something more valuable. He offers His presence.

The study you have in your hands is about learning to seek God's *presence*. We often want His "<u>provision</u>" when God's deepest desire is to share His "<u>presence</u>" with us. May this study in some small way teach you about God and His determination to "be with you".

"...and lo, I am with you always, even to the end of the age."
Matthew 28:20b (NASB)

Chapter 1
Trouble

Storms of Life

One night there was a storm—the kind that lingers. It started with a few flashes and settled into a low rumble. Our four year old grand-daughter was alarmed and then happy. She skipped downstairs to get her pillow, singing as she went. Why so happy? Because when it thunders we let her sleep on the couch in the loft outside our bedroom door. The thing that should have caused her panic and fear was now a source of joy. The presence of the storm meant that she could sleep near us. She can see us, we can see her. Everyone is happy. Within a few minutes she was asleep. The storm continued. She slept on.

It reminded me of someone else who slept through a storm.

"On the evening of that day, he said to them, 'Let us cross over to the other side of the lake.' So they sent the crowd home and took him with them in the little boat in which he had been sitting, accompanied by other small craft. Then came a violent squall of wind which drove the waves aboard the boat until it was almost swamped. Jesus was in the stern asleep on the cushion. They awoke him with the words, 'Master, don't you care that we're drowning?' And he woke up, rebuked the wind, and said to the waves, 'Hush now! Be still!' The wind dropped and everything was very still. 'Why are you so frightened? What has happened to your faith?!', he asked them. But sheer awe swept over them and they kept saying to each other, 'Who ever can he be? – even the wind and the waves do what he tells them!'"　　　　　　　　　　Mark 4:35-41 (Phillips)

I've heard it explained that Jesus slept because he was so exhausted. More importantly, I would argue, he slept because the storm held no fear for Him. He was sleeping with his Father's eye upon Him. There was a demonic storm, but God knew where He was.

As difficulties in my own life come up, I tend, like the disciples, to fear the storm. I forget that my Father's eye is on me. He knows where I am. May I learn to rest in my Father's arms in the midst of the trouble.

Make a simple time line of your life. Use a separate piece of paper if you need to. Make highs and lows with a continuous line to indicate good and bad periods.

Even though Joseph was from a dysfunctional family, he lived a life of integrity. His story can be found in Genesis chapters 37-50. In these chapters, we read several times, "the Lord was with him". He experienced betrayal and hardship, but the Lord was with him.

- The Lord was with him when he was hated by his brothers.
- The Lord was with him when he was sold into slavery.
- The Lord was with him when He worked in Potiphar's house.
- The Lord was with him when he was falsely accused.
- The Lord was with him when he was in jail.
- The Lord was with him when he interpreted the dreams.
- The Lord was with him when he was forgotten by men.
- The Lord was with him when he worked for Pharaoh.

He did nothing to deserve trouble. Yet God was kind to Joseph through the unkind circumstances.

- God was kind to Joseph's family by saving them from the famine.
- God was kind to the Egyptians by saving them from starvation.
- God was kind to Joseph by allowing him to be part of God's plan to bring deliverance.

There is no mention of Joseph doubting God's goodness. There is no hint of bitterness. After the death of his father, Joseph reassures his brothers by telling them, *"...you meant evil against me, but God meant it for good in order to bring about this present result, to preserve many people alive."* Gen. 50:20 (NASB)

Sometimes trouble comes to my life. I don't know why most things happen, but...

- I do know that God is kind.
- I do know that God is sovereign.
- I do know that sometimes God is up to something I don't understand.
- I do know that God is with me.

That simply needs to be enough.

Do you want God's provision more than God's presence?

Read Job 1:1-2:9

1. What do we learn about Job from the first 5 verses? (Possessions and actions). What did he possess? What did he do?

2. Looking at the rest of the passage, what was happening from Job's perspective?

3. What was the bigger story?

4. What perspective did Job's wife see?

In essence she was saying, "God is not good; you trusted Him and look at what it got you. Curse God and die!"

Throughout scripture God promises to be with us. The phrase "[I] will be with you" is used with Abraham, Isaac, Jacob, Joseph, Moses and Joshua. Matthew 1:23 says Jesus will be called, "Immanuel, which translated means, God with us." (NASB) Jesus' last words in Matthew 28:20 were, "Lo, I am with you always, even to the end of the age." (NASB) Finally, in Revelation 21:3, which speaks of eternity future it says, "And I heard a loud voice from the throne saying, 'Behold, the tabernacle of God is among men, and He will dwell among them, and they shall be His people, and God Himself will be among them.'" (NASB) The deepest desire of God's heart is to be with us. In his presence we will find all the provision we will ever need.

Let's continue Job's story. Remember his wife's response? *"Curse God and die."*

5. What was Job's response to her in Job 2:10?

Next, Job had to deal with his well-meaning friends. Their failure to understand the why, led them to blame Job for his circumstances. Job cries out to God who is the only one who completely understands and who is with him in his trouble.

Read Job 42:1-17

6. What happened to Job's perspective in verses 2-6?

7. What does verse 5 mean?

8. What have you learned about God?

9. Where has your thinking been wrong?

10. Take some time to think about these questions.

Turn to page 72 at the back of the book and look at the lament worksheet. Read one or two of the passages listed. You will be working on writing your own lament over the next few days or weeks.

Chapter 2
Honest Emotions

Life is difficult. Sometimes it is downright horrific.

- There are the day to day annoyances: the rude person at the bank, the person who cuts you off in traffic, the lady at the grocery store blocking the aisle.
- There are the heart rending conflicts with people: the spouse who is always critical, the child who is angry that he is part of your family, the friend who "unfriended" you on Facebook, being accused of something unthinkable by someone who should know better.
- There are the life changing difficulties: job loss, divorce, death in the family, sexual abuse.

It does no good to pretend these things don't hurt us. To put on a smile and say "Praise the Lord" does not change what is happening within our hearts. Psalm 51:6 says, "Behold, You desire truth in the innermost being." God knows about these struggles. It isn't wise to try to forget they happen or deny their existence. They need to be faced honestly with God. We should bring these things to Him so He can address them head on.

Own up to the fact that you got mad at the lady in the grocery store, or that you were offended by the rude driver. Only then can God deal with your own selfish heart that puts your own wants and needs before others.

Own up to the fact that when your spouse uses cruel or critical words it wounds you. It cuts you to the core. Own up to the fact that you are devastated that your child doesn't return the love that you so carefully and tirelessly give him. Own up to the fact that you were blindsided by the friend who now appears to be your enemy.

Own up to the fact that losing your job has made you worry about the future, the divorce has shaken your belief that all is right with the world, the death has left you wanting to die yourself and longing for heaven where there is no more death and pain (Revelation 21:4), the sexual abuse has left you doubting the goodness of God in the midst of the memories and betrayal. Only when we are honest can God work to heal the deep scars and sickness.

Define the following:

Stoicism –

Repression –

Sensationalism –

Duplicity –

Hannah and Tamar are examples of emotional honesty. We will look at each one separately.

Hannah – I Samuel 1:1-18

1. Besides God, who were the four main characters?

2. What was the conflict?

3. Why did Peninnah taunt Hannah?

4. What was Hannah's response to the taunting?

5. What was Elkanah's response to Hannah? What was he not getting?

6. Who did Hannah turn to in her grief?

7. What were the three things she asked God for?

8. What did she promise in exchange?

9. What was Eli's initial response to Hannah?

10. What explanation did Hannah give Eli for her behavior?

11. What was Eli's final word to her?

12. What was different about Hannah after she poured out her heart to God?

13. How can you relate to Hannah's story? How would you have responded under the same circumstances?

14. What circumstances in your life have been or are causing you grief? How have you responded? What do you need to change?

Tamar – II Samuel 13:1b-22

1. List the five main characters.

2. What was the inciting incident?

3. What do we know about Jonadab? How is he described?

4. What was his advice to Amnon?

5. Who does Amnon involve in the deception?

6. Was there anything Tamar could have done to avoid this situation?

7. What was Tamar's response to her brother's advances?

8. What was Amnon's response to Tamar after the rape?

9. What was Tamar's response? How did she show emotional honesty?

10. What was Absalom's initial response? What was his hidden response? Did Absalom's failure to act immediately mean he was unaffected? (See 13:23-32)

11. What was David's response?

12. What can you learn from the reactions of those involved?

13. Who do you identify with in this story?

As we consider our own life, we realize we don't have the ability to respond as we should. It is only through the power of Christ that we can move forward with grace and purpose. Philippians 4:6 says,

"Be anxious for nothing, but in everything by prayer and supplication with thanksgiving let your requests be made known to God." (NASB) As we bring these things to God we see the impossible happen. Philippians 4:7 *"And the peace of God, which surpasses all comprehension, will guard your hearts and your minds in Christ Jesus."* (NASB) Verse 8 gives us suggestions on what to set our mind on: *"Finally, brethren, whatever is true, whatever is honorable, whatever is right, whatever is pure, whatever is lovely, whatever is of good repute, if there is any excellence and if anything worthy of praise, dwell on these things."* (NASB)

The point here is not that we are happy about difficulties, but that it is only with God's strength that we can learn to be content, and yes, even joyful in what God is doing in our lives in the midst of trouble.

Trouble will continue to come. It is only through God's grace that we can respond as we should. Honestly turn your face to God and let Him, bit by bit, change your focus, your mindset, and your heart.

Only he who admits he is sick can find healing.

Chapter 3
Grief and Mourning Turn to Hope

<u>Christmas Mourning</u>

How to separate the good from the bad.

Christmas

Be merry when you feel like crying.

Concentrate on Christmas.

Joy to the World...

My Mom just died

The Lord is Come...

She really is better off

Let Earth receive her king...

I had been saying good-bye to her this year already.

Let every heart...

Oh, my heart hurts.

Prepare Him room...

Get ready to celebrate Christmas.

**And heaven and nature sing, and heaven and nature sing,
And heaven and heaven and nature sing.**

Learning to Seek God's Presence

Could God have felt like this that first Christmas?

God's gift meant the death of His Son.

Joy to the World…

His much loved Son would die.

The Lord is Come…

The world would be better off.

Let Earth receive her king…

God was prepared for this. He had planned it.

Let every heart…

Oh, His heart must have hurt.

Prepare Him room…

Get ready to celebrate Christmas.

**And heaven and nature sing, and heaven and nature sing,
And heaven and heaven and nature sing.**

(Karen Pickering – December 2007)

Hagar's story

Read Genesis 16:1-13

1. List the three main characters.

2. Where was Hagar from?

3. What was the problem?

4. What was Sarai's solution?

5. Did Sarai get what she wanted? If so, did it make her happy?

6. What was Sarai's focus?

7. When Hagar was mistreated she fled. Where do you suppose she was headed?

8. Who found Hagar? Was she looking for God?

9. What name does she give God and what does it mean?

Isaac was born fourteen years later. Read Genesis 21:8-21 for the rest of Hagar's story.

Learning to Seek God's Presence

1. List the five main characters.

2. What is the inciting incident?

3. What happens because of it?

4. Where does Hagar go?

5. What does Hagar do when her water runs out?

6. Who heard Hagar and Ishmael?

7. What did the angel tell her?

8. How were their immediate and future needs met?

9. What do you learn about God from these two passages?

10. How does Hagar's life relate to yours?

11. How can you apply these truths to your present circumstances?

David's Example

Read Psalm 56

David, who would later become King of Israel, was living the life of a fugitive. He was beleaguered and in distress because Saul was continually pursuing him and trying to kill him. When he wrote Psalm 56, he had fled to the land of the Philistines, a people with a long history of terrorizing Israel, where he sought to shelter himself from Saul. (I Samuel 21:10-15; 27:4; 29:2-11). In this psalm, he is asking God to make a remembrance of all the suffering he has been through. He is trusting God to eventually vindicate him.

Write out the following verses.

Psalm 56:8

Psalm 6:6

Psalm 42:3

Psalm 126:5

Revelation 7:17

Revelation 21:4

One day we will see our God face to face. On that day, He will take his hand and gently wipe away our tears, and the heavy sadness we have carried will be gone. Our crying will be done.

Other Examples

In speaking of Jesus, Hebrews 5:7 says, *"In the days of His flesh, He offered up both prayers and supplications with loud crying and tears to the One able to save Him from death, and He was heard because of His piety."* (NASB)

Psalm 73 was written by Asaph who was David's chief musician or music director. He probably wrote most of the music for David's Psalms. Take some time to read it now.

1. How does the Psalm begin in verse 1? What is the mood?

2. List 2 or 3 complaints from verses 2-14. Are the complaints you listed accurate or true statements?

3. When we are sad or depressed, can our emotions affect our thinking?

4. What was the turning point in verse 17?

5. What do verses 21 & 22 mean?

6. What was Asaph's hope in verse 23?

7. How does the Psalm end? (vv. 25-28) Are Asaph's troubles over? If not, why the change in attitude?

Chapter 4
Courage under Pressure

The Courage of Sailors

I had always imagined him on a huge navy ship cutting through the ocean toward Europe and the War that was taking place there. My father was a radioman in the navy during World War II. He talked about being sick and doing his job in the very bottom of the boat. Most of his time was spent in Italy. I recently found records that showed the two vessels he was on. They were both LCIs, which stands for Landing Craft, Infantry. The sailors called them "spit-kits." I was startled when I saw pictures of them—they were tiny.

An admiral who saw them swarming around his battleship called them "water bugs". They were only 158' long and 23.3' at their widest. They had a crew of no more than twenty-five. Because of their flat bottom, they were able to do a job the big ships couldn't. They could make quick beach landings. Ramps would be lowered from both sides of the bow, and 200 soldiers would disembark into the shallow waters; total time—ten minutes. The anchor they had dropped while off shore would then pull them back out to sea.

Here is a description from someone who was there.

> "…So we went to sea. The lawyers, the bankers, the garage mechanics, the farmers, the salesmen, and me. In our little spitkits, we struck out boldly if not fearfully…" On the seasickness of the sailors he simply stated, "They've got no guts left, these kids. They've spilled them all. But they've got what it takes. Fine spirit. Game guys. Big men in little ships. American youth, learning the hardest way of all, on the high seas in a spitkit through the war zone. They take it all in stride and somehow (God only knows) they manage to smile. Somehow, also…you go below feeling that's why

31

we'll win this war. No one can beat that kind of stuff!"
(From Samuel Eliot Morison Vol. II – History of United States Naval Operations in World War II – Operations in North African Waters)

Yes, there were big battleships and aircraft carriers. There were supply ships and destroyers, but I believe the war would not have been won without these little LCI's or "water bugs." The LCI's were small and vulnerable; often shot up, bombed, torpedoed and struck by underwater mines. Kamikaze planes used them as targets. These sailors crossed the ocean in vessels that weren't made for crossing the ocean. They were uncomfortable and sick while they did it. They were determined to do what they could, no matter the cost, to stem the tide of evil.

"...but God has chosen the foolish things of the world to shame the wise, and God has chosen the weak things of the world to shame the things which are strong." I Corinthians 1:27 (NASB)

Daniel 3 tells the story of three young Hebrew men; Shadrach, Meshach and Abednego. They were living as exiles in Babylon. Nebuchadnezzar, the king of Babylon, built a golden statue that was ninety feet tall. At the statue's dedication, all the people of the kingdom were gathered, and the command was given to fall down and worship the image when they heard the prearranged music. Those who would not comply were to face immediate death by being thrown into a fiery furnace. Shadrach, Meshach and Abednego refused to bow. Even when they were brought face to face before the enraged king, they would not bow. His threat became reality. They were sent to the fire. Read Daniel 3:17-18.

1. What did they tell the king their God was able to do?

2. What other very real possibility were they aware of?

3. Did the thought that God might not spare them from the fire change their mind about worshiping the king's golden image?

God's presence was more important to them than God's provision.

Hebrews 11 is a wonderful chapter intended to fill us with hope. In it are stories of God working through weak men and women just like us. Read verses 1-34

1. List five of your favorite characters.

2. Why are you drawn to these five people? What about their lives inspires you?

3. Who in those verses can you relate to the most?

Read verses 35-40

1. Make a list of the others mentioned in verses 35-37.

2. The world treated them as if they were not worthy to live, but what does verse 38 say about them?

3. Was God still involved? Is trouble an indication that God is not at work? When stories don't end well does it mean God has abandoned us?

4. Looking at verse 39, who gained approval? How or Why?

5. What does verse 6 say about faith?

6. What have you learned about God?

7. How can you apply these truths to your present circumstances?

Read Jeremiah 17:9 and Mark 7:20-23

1. How is the heart described in Jeremiah?

2. What does Mark say comes out of the heart?

Like many people in this world, you may have experienced something very unpleasant or even horrific. But it is important to remember that what you experience does not make your heart the way it is: sinful, angry, selfish, or self-absorbed. How you react to your circumstances only reveals what was already in your heart. What is in your heart reveals what you believe and who you belong to.

Are you using your past or present circumstances as an excuse for any ungodly behavior? Do you often say, "I can't help it"? Do you think you have been so wounded that you can't help but sin? Do you treat others badly and then try to justify your behavior? Nowhere does Scripture ever excuse sin because of circumstances. You do yourself no favors by avoiding the real problem which is your own wicked and sinful heart. To focus on the wicked and sinful heart of someone who has hurt you shifts the focus off the real problem - your own heart.

*"And the sons of Israel sighed because of the bondage, and they cried out; and their cry for help because of their bondage rose up to God. So **God heard** their groaning; and **God remembered** His covenant with Abraham, Isaac, and Jacob. And God saw the sons of Israel, and **God took notice** of them."* Exodus 2:23b-25 (NASB)

The Israelites were abused as slaves in Egypt for years. God called Moses to lead them out of their bondage. God brought them out with a strong arm and tenderly cared for them in the wilderness. Their response was to complain repeatedly, make a god they liked better, and long to be back in Egypt. They wanted God's provision more than God's presence. God didn't excuse their sin. He didn't say, "Well, it's to be expected, they have been through so much hardship, and they are a broken people; I will just ignore their complaining a little longer." No, He was angry, very angry! He expected their trust and obedience. They were to remember with thanksgiving that God had brought them out of Egypt with a strong arm, and that He delivered them from bondage. Instead of rejoicing in who God is and in what God had done, they were completely focused on themselves and what they didn't have.

35

Learning to Seek God's Presence

The year was 627 B.C. The main political players were Assyria, Egypt and Babylon. Jeremiah, who was called by God to be a prophet at the young age of 17-20, reluctantly agreed despite his inability to speak. God touched his mouth and the impossible became possible. God used him to speak to his people for about 53 years. Much of that time Jeremiah wept. His distress was related to watching the people he loved (the kingdom of Judah) turn from God to the pagan gods they had encountered in Egypt. He wept as he prophesied about the grim future that awaited Judah because of her treachery. Jerusalem would be destroyed and the people taken into captivity by Babylon. He wept as the people repeatedly ignored his warnings to repent and turn from the pagan gods. He was isolated and lonely, preaching a message no one wanted to hear. He was imprisoned as a traitor when he warned against Judah joining forces with Egypt. Only a small remnant of a once glorious kingdom was left. Around 586 B.C., the remnant fled to Egypt and took Jeremiah with them. This passage gave hope that one day God would bring the remnant back. They would be restored, Jerusalem would be rebuilt, and God would be their God.

"Behold, I am bringing them from the north country, and I will gather them from the remotest parts of the earth, among them the blind and the lame ... a great company, they will return here. With weeping they will come, and by supplication I will lead them; I will make them walk by streams of waters, on a straight path in which they will not stumble; for I am a father to Israel ... For the Lord has ransomed Jacob and redeemed him from the hand of him who was stronger than he. They will come and shout for joy on the height of Zion, and they will be radiant over the bounty of the Lord ... and their life will be like a watered garden, and they will never languish again ... for I will turn their mourning into joy and will comfort them and give them joy for their sorrow ... and they will return from the land of the enemy. There is hope for your future, declares the Lord ... For I satisfy the weary ones and refresh everyone who languishes ... as I have watched over them to pluck up, to break down, to overthrow, to destroy and to bring disaster, so I will watch over them to build and to plant, declares the Lord. ... I will put My law

within them and on their heart I will write it; and I will be their God, and they shall be My people. ... For I will forgive their iniquity, and their sin I will remember no more. Thus says the Lord, who gives the sun for light by day and the fixed order of the moon and the stars for light by night, who stirs up the sea so that its waves roar; the Lord of hosts is His name;" Jeremiah 31:8-35 (NASB)

Turn to the lament worksheet and start working on the first couple of questions.

Chapter 5
Worldly Pursuits vs. Godly Pursuits

The Garage

I have always liked climbing. I grew up where the landscape was flatter than an ironing board. I could see as far as the horizon would let me. Oh, but to see just a little farther; to get just a little better vantage point. My father must have seen the glint in my eye as he adjusted the windows which were leaning up against the back of the garage. "I don't want you climbing up on these." "OK", I nodded. He was a kind and fair man who expected his word to be obeyed. It's not that I wanted to defy him, but later, when I was alone, I found myself behind the garage. No, I wasn't magically transported there. I walked with a purpose in mind. I pondered how easy it would be to put one foot on the small windows, reach up a hand to pull up on the taller windows and then just a few inches to the roof edge. I was already climbing ... didn't want to spend too much time in contemplation. I was usually obedient, but the yearning to see farther was more than I wanted to resist. When I heard my mother call me for supper, I quickly climbed down the way I had climbed up. It's somehow always harder to climb down. I caught my inner forearm and received a long nasty scratch.

The next day, as I reached out my hand to get into the car, my Father saw the scratch. "Where did you get that scratch?" "I don't know", I mumbled. Nothing more was ever said. He knew, and I knew. I guess he thought the painful scratch was enough of a punishment. But here it is 45 years later, and I still feel bad about disappointing my Dad.

Idolatry vs. God

The following passage is God talking about Israel. God tenderly cared for them and provided for their needs in the early years of their history. Centuries later, many had wandered far from God: they were deep in idolatry and without true salvation.

Learning to Seek God's Presence

Read Jeremiah 2:2, 5-13

1. Describe Israel's early relationship with God in verse 2.

2. Where were they?

3. What was their condition in verse 5? Why?

4. What had they been through with God according to verse 6?

5. Where did God bring them? (v. 7)

6. What was their response?

7. What two evils did they commit? (v. 13)

8. What is the difference between a fountain and a cistern? Look up the definitions if you aren't sure.

Read Jeremiah 2:18-22

9. When their own cisterns didn't satisfy, where did they turn?

10. What had God done for them according to verse 20?

11. What was their response to what God had done?

12. What did God do in verse 21? (See also Isaiah 5:1-7)

13. What was their response to His care?

14. What does lye and soap represent?

15. Is it effective?

Read Jeremiah 2:25, 27-32

16. In verse 25 they saw their condition. Why didn't they turn?

17. Do we sometimes continue the path we are on even though we know it is hopeless? What keeps us from turning to God instead of to our own idols? What is keeping you from turning to God?

18. In verse 27, when the Israelites found themselves in trouble, what did they demand?

19. Were they repentant?

20. What was God's response?

In the story *Cry the Beloved Country* by Alan Paton, a country pastor travels to the big city of Johannesburg, South Africa to find his son. After many days of searching, he finds him in prison accused of murder. After a heart wrenching conversation with his son, the father comes out of the prison and talks to a fellow pastor who has been helping him search. This is what the father tells him. "I see no shame in him, no pity for those he has hurt. Tears come out of his eyes, but it seems that he weeps only for himself, not for his wickedness, but for his danger. ... I see only his pity for himself, he who has made two children fatherless."

True repentance involves recognizing our own wickedness. False repentance is only concerned with our situation or discomfort.

21. God has tried to get Israel's attention, but their response was not good. What was their view of God in verse 31?

22. Think on what you have learned and ask yourself the following questions. What have I been through? Where has God brought me? Who am I blaming for my past? What have I replaced God with? What am I trusting in? What do I need to repent of?

Do some more work on your lament then read about the life giving, healing water in Ezekiel 47:1-12.

Repentance is not only a change of mind, but also a change of love and longing.

"But I have this against you, that you have left your first love." Revelation 2:4 (NASB)

"Behold, I stand at the door and knock; if anyone hears My voice and opens the door, I will come in to him, and will dine with him, and he with Me." Revelation 3:20 (NASB)

Self or God?

Read Luke 5:30 & 7:36-50.

1. In Luke 5:30, the scribes and Pharisees were grumbling about Jesus eating with sinners. Why do you think the Pharisee in chapter 7 wanted Jesus to dine with him? What were his possible motives?

2. We can gather clues as to his motives by how he treated Jesus. What did he fail to do?

3. What is the modern-day equivalent of that?

4. What did Jesus do when the host failed to welcome Him?

In Luke 4:24, Jesus proclaims Himself a prophet. They might have also been investigating that claim.

5. Did the Pharisee believe Jesus was who he said he was? (v. 39)

6. Why do you think Jesus didn't leave when He was denied the normal courtesies given to guests?

7. Why was the Pharisee angry about the woman?

8. How did Jesus respond to what the Pharisee was thinking?

9. Why was the woman there and when did she arrive? (v. 45)

10. What do you think she was trying to do by her actions?

11. Why was she crying?

12. List the characters in the story Jesus told.

13. Of those listed, who do you relate to?

14. How are you like the woman? How are you like the Pharisee?

15. What did the woman want?

16. What was her response to Christ redeeming her life? What was her focus?

17. What was Simon's focus?

Jesus' focus was not on His place in society or on the acceptance of the religious elite. His agenda was to be about His Father's business; to seek and save the lost.

Chapter 6
How We See Ourselves

Baba's Story

I know a rabbit named Baba. She once had downy, pure white fur and soft pink on the inside of her silky ears. Her eyes were bright and sparkling. She had an orange scarf around her neck. There was a zipper on her underside that opened to a little pocket that carried a tiny baby bunny. Baba came to live with a baby girl with red hair and became her constant companion. Now, when the little girl is tired or afraid, she pulls Baba close to her face and whispers into the soft pink ears. The scarf was lost long ago. Baba's zipper is broken, and the tiny baby bunny has been put away for safe keeping. Her eyes are dull and scratched. Baba has been washed so many times that her permanent color is grey, and her coat is matted and worn. Her ears, once so lovely and plush, are her roughest part. She has been held and dragged and kissed and loved until she is misshapen, stained, and unrecognizable as a rabbit. There was one horrible episode where Baba was lost in a store, and the little girl spent the night crying and worrying about where she was; would she ever see her again. Baba was retrieved the next morning by the girl's mother and was quickly kissed and hugged and cried over with much relief. From that point on, the little girl was more careful with her. She held her tighter when they ventured out.

What is Baba worth? Obviously, she would not even fetch one cent at a garage sale. Most people would throw her away if they found her. But, to one little girl with red hair, Baba's price is far above rubies. Baba would be a very foolish rabbit indeed if she was proud and bragged about how valuable she was. Her value lies only in being loved by a little girl named Ashlee. Without Ashlee, her value is less than nothing. There is nothing good or valuable in Baba ...

For consider your calling, brethren, that there were not many wise according to the flesh, not many mighty, not many noble; but God has chosen the foolish things of the world to shame the wise, and

God has chosen the weak things of the world to shame the things which are strong, and the base things of the world and the despised God has chosen, the things that are not, so that He may nullify the things that are, so that no man may boast before God. But by His doing you are in Christ Jesus, who became to us wisdom from God, and righteousness and sanctification, and redemption, so that, just as it is written, *"LET HIM WHO BOASTS, BOAST IN THE LORD."* I Corinthians 1:26-31 (NASB)

God doesn't love me because I am valuable; I am valuable because God loves me.

Our focus needs to shift from self to God; therefore, I've chosen not to address self-esteem in this study. God esteem is more important.

Lies We Believe

"Life is bad." "God is bad." "You are bad." "These bad things are happening because God keeps score and isn't happy with you." Here is an even more dangerous lie. "You don't need God, you don't need anyone: you are amazing and self-sufficient."

If I believe any of these lies, I either try self-improvement, which is futile, or I am self-deceived. I choose not to see my desperate need when my only hope is God.

We can choose to trust ourselves with our limited perspective, or we can choose to trust God with His unrestricted pristine perspective.

1. Write out Romans 12:3.

There are two extremes: self-hatred or belittling of self and self-embellishment or worship of self. Both are sinful.

2. Who am I? How do I describe myself?

3. Give examples of self-hatred and self-worship. Make the lists specific to you.

4. There are two lists at the back on pages 75 and 76. "Who is God" and "Who am I". They each have a few passages to get you started. Continue to fill them in with information you learn from this study and other Bible reading.

"If then you have been raised up with Christ, keep seeking the things above, where Christ is seated at the right hand of God. Set your mind on the things above, not on the things that are on earth. For you have died and your life is hidden with Christ in God. When Christ, who is our life, is revealed, then you also will be revealed with Him in glory. Therefore consider the members of your earthly body as dead to immorality, impurity, passion, evil desire, and greed which amounts to idolatry." Colossians 3:1-5 (NASB)

5. Where do I need to adjust my thinking? Pray about having an accurate view of yourself.

A Parable

Read Luke 18:9-14

1. Who was Jesus talking to in verse 9?

2. List the two main characters in this parable.

3. What was the focus of the Pharisee's prayer? What did he ask God for?

4. Circle every time the word "I" is used in verses 11 & 12.

5. What was he thankful for?

6. Where was the tax-gatherer standing?

7. What could he boast of before God?

8. What did he ask God for?

9. Who was outwardly a better man? (see note)

10. Who went home justified?

11. Who do you relate to in the story? Why?

(Note: Tax-gatherers were considered traitors. They were collecting money from the local people to help fund the occupying Roman army. They were considered thieves and were not accepted in society.)

Self-focus doesn't lead to Godliness.

"Stop regarding man, whose breath of life is in his nostrils; for why should he be esteemed?" Isaiah 2:22 (NASB)

Read Jeremiah 17:5-6

1. Describe the man in these verses.

2. Draw a picture of his environment. If you don't feel comfortable drawing, find a picture in a magazine or on the internet that fits the description.

Read Jeremiah 17:7-8

3. Describe the man in these verses.

4. Draw a picture of his environment. Again, if you don't feel comfortable drawing, find a picture in a magazine or on the internet that fits the description.

Read Galatians 5:13-15

5. What problem is mentioned in Galatians?

6. What is the result of self-focus?

Chapter 7
Wrong View of Others

The Bully in All of Us

I was seven. My mother gave me a rare birthday party that didn't involve just family. I was allowed to invite three friends. One was a shy little waif who lived down the road from us. She was a year or two younger than I was. She came, but didn't speak. We played a game that involved breaking balloons. She couldn't bring herself to break hers and carried it home intact like a trophy that would sit carefully on a shelf.

She must have had a good time, because, for the next two weeks, she followed me around the school playground whenever I was out. She never said anything, just silently followed. Elementary school is all about image and ranking order. Having a little first grader following me around didn't enhance my image.

After two weeks, I had had enough. I suddenly turned around and burst out, "Quit following me!" She immediately stopped, looked down and hurried away.

Girls can be so cruel. We watch injustice and determine to make a difference or to "save" the lost soul, and yet the reality isn't as romantic.

It still makes me sick to think about it. I should have run after her. I should have apologized. I should have been the friend she needed me to be. Instead, I muttered something to my friends about how irritating she was. I was too busy worshiping the god of self to be bothered with her. I don't remember what kind of reaction my companions had. I don't even remember who they were. But I can still remember my neighbor and the lesson she taught me that day without even speaking a word.

"We love, because He first loved us. If someone says, 'I love God,' and hates his brother, he is a liar; for the one who does not love his brother whom he has seen, cannot love God whom he has not seen. And this commandment we have from Him: that the one who loves God should love his brother also." I John 4:19-21 (NASB)

How do you interact with others? Are you others-centered like God, or am self-centered like Cain? (Genesis 4:1-15) Do I have a deep seated idolatry; myself being my focus and my own god? Do you tend to be fueled by a drive that uses others for your own well-being instead of serving others for their well-being?

Some bad examples

Read II Samuel 11-12:25

1. Where should David have been? (v. 1)

2. Who should have been his focus?

3. What was his focus and what did it lead to?

4. Who suffered because of David's sin?

Read Genesis 29 as background and then answer the following questions from Genesis 30:1-3.

5. What was Rachel's focus?

6. What did she want and from whom?

7. How did she treat him?

8. What was Jacob's response? (30:2)

9. What did her envy lead to?

Read the following verses that apply to us and our own circumstances.

"What is the source of quarrels and conflicts among you? Is not the source your pleasures that wage war in your members? You lust and do not have; so you commit murder. And you are envious and cannot obtain; so you fight and quarrel. You do not have because you do not ask. You ask and do not receive, because you ask with wrong motives, so that you may spend it on your pleasures. You adulteresses, do you not know that friendship with the world is hostility toward God? Therefore whoever wishes to be a friend of the world makes himself an enemy of God." James 4:1-4 (NASB)

"But if you bite and devour one another, take care lest you be consumed by one another!" Galatians 5:15 (NASB)

"Be of sober spirit, be on the alert. Your adversary, the devil, prowls around like a roaring lion seeking someone to devour." I Peter 5:8 (NASB)

Read the following passage from Luke, make the markings suggested and then answer the questions. Note: Jesus was addressing the Pharisees (Luke 16:14-15) who were the religious elite of his day.

"Once there was a rich man who used to dress in purple and fine linen and live in great luxury every day. A beggar named Lazarus, who was covered with sores, was brought to his gate. He was always trying to satisfy his hunger with what fell from the rich man's table. Even (but) the dogs used to come and lick his sores. One day the beggar died and was carried away by the angels to Abraham's side. The rich man also died and was buried. In the afterlife, where he was in constant torment, he looked up and saw Abraham far away and Lazarus by his side. So he shouted, 'Father Abraham, have mercy on me! Send Lazarus to dip the tip of his finger in water to cool off my tongue, because I am suffering in this fire.' But Abraham said, 'My child, remember that during your lifetime you received blessings, while Lazarus received hardships. But now he is being comforted here, while you suffer. Besides all this, a wide chasm has been fixed between us, so that those who want to cross from this side to you cannot do so, nor can they cross from your side to us.' The rich man said, 'Then I beg you, father, send Lazarus to my father's house- because I have five brothers-to warn them, so that they won't end up in this place of torture too.' Abraham said, 'They have Moses and the Prophets. They should listen to them!' But the rich man replied, 'No, father Abraham! But if someone from the dead went to them, they would repent.' Then Abraham told him, 'If your brothers do not listen to Moses and the Prophets, they will not be persuaded, even if someone were to rise from the dead.'" Luke 16:19-31 (ISV)

Choose three different pen or pencil colors. Use the first one for the rich man, the second one for Lazarus and the third one for Abraham. Circle the name or pronoun referring to each character with the appropriate color.

1. Contrast the rich man's and Lazarus' circumstances while on earth.

2. Who was the rich man focused on?

3. Lazarus was brought to the rich man's gate. Who do you suppose brought him there and why?

4. What kindness did the dogs show Lazarus? (The Greek word should be translated "but" to show the contrast.)

The dogs mentioned here were more than likely wild guard dogs kept to protect the rich man's property. He probably had an outer gate where Lazarus would have been laid. Inside the gate would have been an inner courtyard and then the actual house. Dogs lick their own wounds and they also lick people as a sign of affection. They knew Lazarus well enough that they didn't think of him as a threat and instead treated him as a friend.

5. Contrast Lazarus' and the rich man's circumstances after death.

6. Notice the rich man mentions Lazarus by name. What does that indicate?

7. What two requests did the rich man make?

8. Who did he want to fulfill those requests?

9. Why didn't he address Lazarus directly instead of asking Abraham?

10. If you were Lazarus what would your response have been? Does Lazarus respond?

11. What does the rich man's condescending attitude toward Lazarus tell you about his frame of mind? Was he repentant?

12. Who was the rich man still focused on?

Attitude Adjustment Worksheet

1. What do I want that I don't have?

2. What do I have that I don't want?

3. How do I typically go about manipulating others?

4. How do I respond to or retaliate against others when they don't seem to come through for me?

5. What would it be like to be in a relationship with me?

6. Do I live to feed, nourish, shepherd, and care for others or do I live to get others to take care of me?

7. What do I need to repent of?

8. Write out a prayer of repentance to God.

9. How do I need to change? Ask God to show you specific goals for change in your life.

Chapter 8
Right View of Others

Now we will be looking at some examples of Godly interactions with others.

Ruth

Read Ruth 1-4. What was Ruth's focus in the following verses?

1. Ruth 1:16-17

2. Ruth 2:11

3. Ruth 3:11

4. Ruth 4:15

5. Contrast Ruth's attitude with Naomi's attitude.

Moses

Exodus 5:1-23

1. What was the specific request God told Moses to ask Pharaoh? (v. 1)

2. What is Pharaoh's response? (vv. 10-21)

3. What does Moses do? Who is he concerned about? (vv. 22-23)

Exodus 32:1-35

4. What does God want to do to the people? (vv. 9-10)

5. What is Moses response? What arguments does he give? What does he remind God of? (vv. 11-13)

6. What does Moses ask God to do as he pleads for the people? (vv. 30-32)

Exodus 33:1-17

7. God is willing to fulfill his promise to give the people the land of Canaan, but what is He refusing to do and why? (vv. 3-4)

8. Does Moses agree to God's conditions? What arguments does he give? (vv. 12-16)

God was offering His provision without His presence. God's presence was finally more important to the people than God's provision.

Paul

"For I could wish that I myself were accursed, separated from Christ for the sake of my brethren, my kinsmen according to the flesh."
Romans 9:3 (NASB)

1. What was Paul willing to do for his kinsmen?

Jesus

"So when He had washed their feet, and taken His garments and reclined at the table again, He said to them, 'Do you know what I have done to you? You call Me Teacher and Lord; and you are right, for so I am. If I then, the Lord and the Teacher, washed your feet, you also ought to wash one another's feet. For I gave you an example that you also should do as I did to you. Truly, truly, I say to you, a slave is not greater than his master, nor is one who is sent greater than the one who sent him. If you know these things, you are blessed if you do them.'" John 13:12-17 (NASB)

1. We usually do not experience immediate or apparent benefits by serving others, so why should we do it? (See I John 4:10-11, 19-21)

2. Who gives us the ability to love and serve others well?
(See Colossians 1:9-11; Ephesians 3:16-20; Philippians 2:13)

Some final words of encouragement.

"And let us consider how to stimulate one another to love and good deeds, not forsaking our own assembling together, as is the habit of some, but encouraging one another; and all the more as you see the Day drawing near." Hebrews 10:24-25 (NASB)

"Do nothing from selfishness or empty conceit, but with humility of mind let each of you regard one another as more important than himself; do not merely look out for your own personal interests, but also for the interests of others." Philippians 2:3-4 (NASB)

"Be devoted to one another in brotherly love; give preference to one another in honor:" Romans 12:10 (NASB)

Look back at question 9 on your Attitude Adjustment Worksheet. Is there anything you would like to add?

Finish writing your lament using the Lament Worksheet and Lament Outline.

Read your lament out loud to God. Share your lament with at least one other person.

Chapter 9
Restoration Process

My Grandmother's Chair

I have two chairs that my grandparents received on their wedding day. They are tiny by today's standards. I used them as thrones when I was a little girl. There was a matching loveseat that I spent hours sprawled out in reading the World Book Encyclopedia. The loveseat met an unfortunate end when it got in the way of a semi-truck, but that is another story.

The chairs were given to me before my mother died. They were the only things I owned that had belonged to my grandmother. About 10 years ago one of the chairs was damaged while being used in a drama production; the front leg and part of the frame were shattered. I couldn't bear to throw it away, so it sat in my basement. I looked at it every once in a while and tried to see if I could fix it. It just seemed impossible because there were too many pieces. Still, I couldn't throw it away. I placed the chair that wasn't damaged beside it; I thought they should be together.

A couple of years ago, I decided to buy some fabric and recover the good one. I bought enough for two chairs just in case. I started on the broken one first. I took out the old tacks, peeled back the old fabric, took out the stuffing and removed the webbing from the bottom. It was looking worse than ever. The springs had come loose, and the leg and frame looked hopeless. I carefully took the leg apart where it met the frame. I cleaned out the old glue. I fit the pieces back together with new glue in the joints, and I added wood filler where the wood was damaged and splintered. I bound it up tight while the glue dried. I also put some braces up inside where they wouldn't show. I sanded and covered up the scratches with stain.

Next, I started putting new webbing on the bottom, retying the springs, layering the burlap, stuffing, cotton cloth, more stuffing, more cotton cloth, and finally the finishing fabric. The braid went on last to cover all the edges. I stepped back and looked it over. I was amazed. It was beautiful! It was also strong ... stronger than it had ever been. I recovered the good chair too. I had to redo some of the stuffing, but I didn't have to touch the springs or the webbing. They were a matched set again. They looked the same, but one was much stronger. The one that had been broken, seemingly beyond usefulness, was now the stronger of the two.

My thoughts turned to people. Many are broken and shattered. As broken people we have two choices. We can hide in the basement and expect other people to stay there with us, or we can offer our broken and shattered pieces to the One who made us. It will hurt. He will have to take things apart, scrape off things that shouldn't be there, and dig out some rotten bits. But, as we trust Him to work with our life, He will make us beautiful and strong: stronger than we would have been if we had never been broken.

"For we are His workmanship, created in Christ Jesus for good works, which God prepared beforehand, that we should walk in them." Ephesians 2:10 (NASB)

Life Change

"You shall love the LORD your God with all your heart and with all your soul and with all your might." Deuteronomy 6:5 (NASB)

Read Mark 10:17-30

1. List the verbs in verse 17 that have to do with the man.

2. What do those verbs indicate about his frame of mind?

3. How did Jesus answer his question? (v. 19)

4. What was the man's response?

5. What was Jesus getting at in verse 21?

The young man was looking for a list. Jesus blew his list out of the water and gave him a life changing option. It was an all or nothing proposition.

6. What was the man's response? How would you have responded?

7. What is the only way any of us can be saved?

8. Peter, with a bit of pride, points out that they had left everything to follow Christ. How did Jesus respond to him? (vv. 29-30)

Paul was even more extreme in actual devotion than the young man mentioned above. Read his background information in Philippians 3:4-11.

1. List his religious qualifications from verses 5 and 6.

This verse sums up his central focus.

"For I determined to know nothing among you except Jesus Christ and Him crucified." I Corinthians 2:2 (NASB)

He was no stranger to hardship. The choice he had made changed his whole life.

Read II Corinthians 4:7-11, 16-18.

2. What was Paul relying on to live his life? (v. 7)

3. List the 6 things that are contrasted from verses 8-11.

4. In the midst of such difficulties, why was Paul not discouraged? (v. 16)

5. What is contrasted in verse 17?

6. What do you learn about things seen and things not seen in verse 18?

Like the rich young man, we all want to know what to do. To follow Christ is simple, yet hard. We are to give our all and yet, the power to live a life pleasing to God comes from God and not from us. There is the paradox of dying so that we can live.

Chapter 10
Non Nobis Domine (Not to Us Oh Lord)

The following speech is from Shakespeare's Henry V. While the play is fictional, it is based on an actual event, the Battle of Agincourt in 1415. King Henry had crossed the English Channel with 10,000 men to get back disputed lands from France. He lost a third of his men to sieges and disease. They had marched over 250 miles in 15 days. They were cut off by about 30,000 French troops and they had only about 6,000 men. They needed a miracle. His men were discouraged and Henry gives this speech to give them courage for the coming battle. (I would recommend that you watch a clip of the speech on the internet. Search for "Henry V St. Crispin's Day Speech".)

Henry V Act 4, Scene 3
Gloucester – Where is the king?
Bedford – The king himself is rode to view their battle.
Westmoreland – Of fighting men they have full threescore thousand.
Exeter – There's five to one. Besides, they all are fresh.
Salisbury – God's arm strike with us! 'Tis a fearful odds. God be with you, princes all. (Talk of heaven etc.)
Westmoreland - Oh, that we now had here (Henry enter) but one ten thousand of those men in England that do no work today.
King Henry V – What's he that wishes so? My cousin Westmoreland? No, my fair cousin.
If we are marked to die, we are enough
To do our country loss; and if to live,
The fewer men the greater share of honor.
God's will, I pray thee wish not one man more. ...For the best hope I have. Oh, do not wish one more!
Rather proclaim it, Westmoreland, through my host,
That he which hath no stomach to this fight,
Let him depart. His passport shall be made,
And crowns for convoy put into his purse.
We would not die in that man's company

That fears his fellowship to die with us.
This day is called the feast of Crispian.
He that outlives this day and comes safe home,
Will stand o' tiptoe when the day is named
And rouse him at the name of Crispian.
He that shall see this day, and live old age,
Will yearly on the vigil feast his neighbors
And say, "Tomorrow is Saint Crispian."
Then will he strip his sleeve and show his scars,
And say, "These wounds I had on Crispin's day."
Old men forget; yet all shall be forgot
But he'll remember with advantages
What feats he did that day. Then shall our names,
Familiar in his mouth as household words,
Harry the king, Bedford and Exeter,
Warwick and Talbot, Salisbury and Gloucester,
Be in their flowing cups freshly remembered.
This story shall the good man teach his son,
And Crispin Crispian shall ne'er go by,
From this day to the ending of the world,
But we in it shall be remembered-
We few, we happy few, we band of brothers;
For he today that sheds his blood with me
Shall be my brother; be he ne'er so vile,
This day shall gentle his condition;
And gentlemen in England now abed
Shall think themselves accursed they were not here,
And hold their manhoods cheap whiles any speaks
That fought with us upon Saint Crispin's day.

According to Shakespeare, only 29 Englishmen died while the
French lost 6,000 to 10,000 soldiers.

Henry V Act 4 Scene 8

King Henry V: This note doth tell me of ten thousand French
That in the field lie slain. (List of dead)
Where is the number of our English dead?

Herald shows him another paper

Edward the Duke of York, the Earl of Suffolk,
Sir Richard Ketly, Davy Gam, esquire;
None else of name, and of all other men
But five and twenty. O God, thy arm was here,
And not to us but to thy arm alone
Ascribe we all! When, without stratagem,
But in plain shock and even play of battle,
Was ever known so great and little loss
On one part and on th' other? Take it, God,
For it is none but thine.
Exeter: 'Tis wonderful.
King Henry V: Come, go we in procession to the village,
And be it death proclaimed through our host
To boast of this or take that praise from God
Which is His only.
Fluellen: Is it not lawful, an please your Majesty,
To tell how many is killed?
King Henry V: Yes, Captain, but with this acknowledgement:
That God fought for us.
Fluellen: Yes, my conscience, He did us great good.
King Henry V: Do we all holy rites.
Let there be sung *Non Nobis* and *Te Deum*,
The dead with charity enclosed in clay,
And then to Calais, and to England then,
Where ne'er from France arrived more happy men.

"Not to us, O LORD, not to us, But to Thy name give glory." Psalm 115:1a (NASB)

Conclusion

Read Hebrews 12:1-3

1. What cloud of witnesses is this passage talking about? (Remember Hebrews 11)

2. What are the three things this passage tells us to do?

3. What three things did Jesus do?

4. Why did He do it?

5. Why should we consider Him?

"Remember your leaders (those who led you – NASB), those who spoke to you the word of God. Consider the outcome of their way of life, and imitate their faith." Hebrews 13:7 (ESV)

We have seen examples of many saints over the last weeks. They have led the way for us. Learn by their example; consider the outcome of their faith and be changed by it.

We must not be discouraged by the overwhelming odds we face; instead, we must remember the strong arm of our God who is with us and who fights for us. Just as the weary English returned home triumphant, we too will be ushered into the presence of His glory triumphant if we hold out our hope firmly unto the end and continue to fight. On the Day of His appearing, we will be delighted that He allowed us to be part of the bigger story. Don't settle. Don't simply survive. Fight! Battle! Take risks! Live, really live!

Look up II Timothy 4:6-8 and write it below.

Consider what you've learned over the last few weeks. How has your thinking changed? How is your life different than it was 10 weeks ago? Pray with your discipleship partner about the ongoing work God is doing in your life. Be encouraged: God is with you!

Softball and being chosen

Softball was my least favorite sport. It had a lot to do with how the game started ... choosing sides. I was little and skinny and usually chosen last. As I grew, my coordination became worse which made me even more undesirable as a teammate. The only time I wasn't chosen last was if there was someone smaller and skinnier than I was. It didn't happen often. On rare occasions, one of the captains happened to be my Dad. I can still hear him saying, "I choose Karen!" Not with reluctance, but with love and confidence. He chose me, not because of my great athletic ability, but because he loved me and wanted me on his team.

That's how it is with God. I Thessalonians 1:4 says, *"Knowing brethren beloved by God, His choice of you."* (NASB) God has picked me! I'm weak and sinful and mess up often, but He loves me and wants me on His team. How can I help but love and serve such a God?

Lament Worksheet

Allow a word of caution before you begin. I want to encourage you to be honest and open with God; He already knows what is in your heart. Keep in mind however, that you are addressing His Sovereign Majesty, the God and Creator of the universe. He is worthy of all reverence and respect. Also, know that He might not answer you as you expect, and, like Job, he might answer your questions with more questions. Yet, He is your Father and wants you to live in His very real presence in the here and now.

See Psalm 13, 22, 28, 55 or 69 for examples. (See also Hezekiah in Isaiah 37:16-20; Jacob in Genesis 32:9-12; Moses in Numbers 11:11-15) Answer the questions below.

Have you been through a crisis situation or some life changing event? What have you lost as a result of what happened? Be as thorough as possible. Don't minimize the loss, don't pretend there wasn't a loss, be honest in your assessment. What do you still struggle with?

Bring this list to God. Tell Him what you are thinking. Face this with Him. Cry out to Him. Ask Him any questions you have been afraid to ask.

Be quiet before God. Let His Word speak to you.

Take the things you have written here and write your own lament psalm. Use the outline on the next page as a guide.

Lament Outline

1. Address God - This is no time for formal titles. This is a time to get face to face and personal. Cry out to Him using a name that makes Him feel accessible to you.

2. Complaint – Describe your anguish. Describe the situation. Describe your fears. Be specific. Use imagery to describe if possible.

3. Petition or Supplication – Urge God to act, to hear, and to deal with the situation.

4. Motivation – Give God reasons why He should act on your behalf. These could include:
> a. God's reputation is at stake.
> b. God acted before, He should act again to be consistent.
> c. Your own guilt
> d. Your own innocence
> e. Promise of praise
> f. Your helplessness
> g. Your trust in Him

It is not disrespectful to petition God. You are coming to Him and speaking this way because you believe in God's ability to act. You believe your life is in His hands and only His hands.

5. Assurance that God has heard.
What good can you see in your life now? What good can you imagine God will do? When it comes right down to it, what do you want more than anything? What does God want more than anything?

6. Singing of praise and thanksgiving – The situation and/or attitude is transformed.

7. Paying of promised vows – How will you function differently because of what has transpired?

Who is God?

Look up the following "You Are" and "I Am" verses about God and write down what you learn. Add more information as you find it.

You Are:

Job 26:2
Psalm 5:4
Psalm 16:2
Psalm 22:3
Psalm 23:4
Psalm 25:5
Psalm 31:3
Psalm 31:4
Psalm 32:7

I Am:
Genesis 15:1
Genesis 26:24
Genesis 28:15
Genesis 35:11
Exodus 6:6
Exodus 22:27
Exodus 29:46
Exodus 31:13
John 6:35, 48, 51
John 8:12, 9:5
John 8:23
John 10:7, 9
John 10:11, 14
John 10:36
John 11:25
John 14:6
John 14:10, 11
John 15:1, 5
John 17:16
John 18:37

Who Am I?

Look up the passages and write down what you learn. Continue to add to the list as you learn more.

You Are:

Matthew 5:13
Matthew 5:14
Matthew 10:31
John 15:5
John 15:14
John 15:19
I Corinthians 3:9
I Corinthians 3:16
I Corinthians 6:19

Bibliography

Bailey, Kenneth E. Jesus Through Middle Eastern Eyes. Downers Grove: Inter Varsity Press, 2008.

Brueggemann, Walter. The Psalms and the Life of Faith. Minneapolis: Augsburg Fortress, 1995.

Card, Michael. A Better Freedom. Downers Grove: Inter Varsity Press, 2009.

—. A Sacred Sorrow. Colorado Springs: NavPress, 2005.

Edwards, Robert Kellemen & Karole A. Beyond the Suffering. Grand Rapids: Baker Books, 2007.

Holy Bible - New American Standard Bible. La Habra: The Lockman Foundation, 1977.

Johnston, Wayne A. Mack and Wayne Erick. A Christian Growth and Discipleship Manual. Bemidji: Focus Publishing, n.d.

Kellemen, Robert W. Soul Physicians. Winona Lake: BMH Books, 2007.

MacDonald, William. Believer's Bible Commentary. Nashville: Thomas Nelson Publishers, 1995.

Paton, Alan. Cry, The Beloved Country. New York: Charles Scribner's Sons, 1948.

Tchividjian, Tullian. Surprised by Grace. Wheaton: Crossway, 2010.

Author's website: www.lytrooretreat.wordpress.com
If you have any questions about the material please contact me at bkpickering@gmail.com

Made in United States
North Haven, CT
02 June 2023

37240981R00046